THE STEAMING SIXTIES
Stirring episodes from the last decade of Steam on BR
8. LMR: London and the North
Euston to St Pancras via Yorkshire
Or: A Tale of Two Cup Finals...

By Robin Charlton
Photographs A.G. Forsyth, Initial Photographics

Copyright Irwell Press,
ISBN 978-1-906919-26-9
First published in 2010 by Irwell Press Ltd., 59A, High Street, Clophill, Bedfordshire, MK45 4BE
Printed by Konway Press.

As 1964 wore on the glories of Euston, the courtly Great Hall, the statuary, the pillars, the marvellous propylaeum of the Euston Arch, had all been torn down, gouged out and made hideous; a high-water mark of the stupid and arrogant post-war belief that 'Victorian' was backward and actually *deserving* of obliteration. So was the capital's first terminus, the first anywhere in the world and built to proclaim the glory of engineering, commerce and empire, demolished to provide instead a not even mediocre office block damned as often as not by howling winds and cursed by tramps, litter and the debris of fast food. Instead of the Euston Arch proclaiming the place as gateway to the North we have a sprawling, ugly and chaotic bus stop at its front. But with our period, *The Steaming Sixties*, we are necessarily dealing with lost glory; on 9 May 1964 *(right)*, with much of the old place ripped open to the sky, a nevertheless smart Black Five, 45379, stands on what looks like the old Platform 1, on 9 May 1964; the work has opened up the east side of the station and we can see all the way through to Eversholt Street, the thoroughfare running north at that side. At one period, in June 1964, the station was largely closed for days on end, with trains diverted to other London termini.

Saturday 9 May 1964 was Rugby League Final day and specials had filtered up to town, often in the hands of Jubilees, from the Friday, later accumulating at Willesden shed for servicing. Crewe North turned out this Black Five, 44762, for special 1T91; left, it is descending Camden Bank for the run into the terminus and later (right) its train has been taken away and it has reversed to the platform end, awaiting the signal to

run out to Willesden shed for servicing. It was always noticeable at Euston (compared to Kings Cross, say) how often so little was going on at the platform end. You never got the 'hordes' here that you got a little bit further down the Euston Road.

The early 1960s saw Coronation Pacifics replaced by English Electric Type 4s. This made life a lot easier for crews who welcomed the more comfortable life, without the physical effort, and who could blame them? The drawback was that the new locomotives were plagued by technical deficiencies (the harsh winter of 1962-63 showed the entire hurried dieselisation project in a properly dismal light) and, moreover, they were underpowered for the job in hand. Why on earth vastly powerful Pacifics, probably the best ever developed in this country, had to be replaced wholesale for an interim period of just two or three years before electrification seems beyond reason now. Why the LMR could not have muddled through with steam for a little longer without the vast expense of dieselisation is one of those 'why did we do that?' questions that will never now be answered. Well, every picture tells a story, and here is Willesden's 73039 (the shed by now did all the pilot work at the terminus; it always had done in terms of empty stock, with Camden providing 3F 0-6-0Ts for the pottering about side of things) removing an EE Type 4 which had given up the ghost on arrival at Platform 1, in November 1963.

Willesden, 1A, in July 1965. The grand old shed sat between the main line and the canal to the south; you didn't appreciate it at the time but it had once been twice as long, the later (front, and more youthful) portion of roofing having gone the way of all flesh and in true railway fashion the locos had simply stood in the open ever since. 8F 2-8-0 48084 hailed from Stourton, one of the Leeds sheds; it would be fairly safe to say that there weren't that many North Eastern Region engines in West London that day.

Prominent towards the end at Willesden were the BR 78000 2-6-0s and in July 1965 there are two visible on the left; the nearest one is 78029. A type barely known there for many years, eight or so were unexpectedly came to the old place in May 1963, garnered from distant sheds, mainly in the North West. Two years later another half dozen arrived. There had been a long tradition, going back to LNW days, of working the Euston empty stock, particularly on the long run out to Stonebridge park, with old timers of every description, from elderly 0-6-2Ts to ancient ex-Midland 2F 0-6-0s. These had all long gone by the 1960s, when the work was done by anything Willesden could dig up, it seemed. The 78000s proved popular with the crews, and the cab was particularly appreciated on a job that involved both running in reverse for half the time as well as a lot of standing around, often in a nippy side wind.

Willesden deeper back in the steam age, when even the EE Type 4s weren't yet dominant on the LNW, on 13 May 1961. Poor old 'Super D' 0-8-0 49413, to be officially withdrawn later that year, in October, looks already done for, without shed plate, covered in rust and with that strange totem on the top lamp iron. Electrification was in the air of course, though it was still far off in the North West at this time. Nevertheless it was important to imbue all staff with an awareness of the hazards of the overhead line (OHL) and at Willesden, as at many other sheds, an OHL mock-up was made to demonstrate the clearances that would have to be observed. Hence the locally knocked-up masts and line shown here, with an engine of a type that would be banned under the wires in any event. Dear old 49413 officially went for scrap in November 1962 though it is hard to imagine it did any work after this.

In the London suburbs, 1963. Black Five 45215 is heading north under the Headstone Lane bridge on newly ballasted track; it is an Annesley engine, and thus not exactly a common sight in these parts. It has found its way to London, despatched thence by Crewe South as part of its running in and now Willesden has taken advantage of an unexpected 'spare'. Observe how busy the little goods yard still is, even this late on, especially with domestic coal. The prominent brick building is one of the sub-stations erected for the LNW electric 'New Line' serving Watford, just visible to the right. The platforms of the Headstone Lane station, which served only the new electric lines (on which Bakerloo Line trains were later extended) are just visible through the bridge. When the 'Watford DC' was ready throughout in 1922 the line at Headstone Lane ran through fields with only scattered houses. It was hoped that 'a modern garden suburb' would spring up in the wake of the new electric service but what grew up was a conventional suburb of the period, indistinguishable from many another.

The first water troughs out of Euston were at Bushey which had an unsuspected significance, so near were they to the terminus. Euston was not well provided for with respect to water columns, and a lot could be used up getting from Camden to the station to take a down train while it could also run short after arrival there, in the hour or more it might take to get back out to Camden shed and salvation. So it was that often, a crew of an up train would take pains to ensure a full tender on the way in, while a crew of a down working would need a good, early, top up. On 23 April 1962 Stanier Pacific 46253 CITY OF ST ALBANS hurries up to town on the up fast, though the opportunity to take water seems to have been declined. On the left are our old friends the Watford DC lines.

On the same day, 23 April 1962, 2-6-4T 42066 hurries south on the up slow; the brake van of a down freight vanishes in the distance. The two Bakerloo Line/Watford DC lines are on the left – one of them through that extra arch forged in the Oxhey Road bridge, giving it an asymmetrical look. Water troughs were dangerous places for anyone with business on the track, as bad as tunnels in many respects; note, for instance, the little refuge just in front of 42066. Clearances were tight and underfoot it was almost permanently wet and slimy and therefore treacherous. Engines taking water frequently 'overflowed' and half a ton of water at even a modest speed let alone the lumps of coal it might carry off a tender could kill.

By 1964 the old LNW was truly a line in transition, and not always a happy one. It had a diesel passenger service, worked by underpowered and not wholly reliable locos with endless disruption due to engineering work as the masts and wire went up and bridge after bridge was demolished and rebuilt. Freight, on the other hand, was largely in the hands of steam; this traffic too was disrupted by the same engineering work and the locomotives, entering the last year or so of their lives, were often neglected and not at their best. With so much civil engineering work underway there were plenty of 'ballasts' to be worked and amid the drastically changing railscape here is one in September 1964, inching through Bletchley behind 8F 2-8-0 48467.

The towns along the line with engine sheds, such as Bletchley, remained shrinking islands of steam as the main line alongside was transformed out of all recognition. For a long time Bletchley was a vast building site with upheaval all around as, along with the electrification itself, the station was rebuilt into anonymous concrete modernity. Traditions nonetheless lingered on, such as the 3F tank on station pilot duty; a dirt-black 47521, pilot lamps up, was fussing with stock in September 1964. Two were usually in use; 47521 had been on and off the job most of the year in fact, and survived into 1966.

Up freight, tanks and Presflos, north of Bletchley station in September 1964, behind a 9F 2-10-0, unidentifiable under the filth. The footbridge is of interest; obviously on the left the stairway is original, with a later extension to the right. It was tall enough to avoid demolition for the OHL (overhead line). Observe the easy attitude of the spotters, conversing almost with the fireman. That big sign doubtless proclaims the onset of modernisation in the area.

North of Bletchley station in September 1964 and Black Five 44945 has a down class 4 freight amid a cloud of black smoke. By this time, with the ban 'south of Crewe' on some former LMS types, the Duchesses, Scots and Jubilees were largely in the past, but Britannias had become common instead, as they all found their way on to the LMR.

Presumably working to the shed, a pair of 8Fs, 48077 in front, pause in the platform at Bletchley in September 1964. The place was being progressively remodelled amid much upheaval and a bewildering forest of mastwork was sprouting everywhere; the new footbridge and its lifts in the background came into use earlier in the year.

Looking north from the new footbridge in September 1964 as an errant Jubilee, 45672 ANSON officially banned from the 1st of the month, rumbles light below. The image of a 'forest' of masts is seen to be an apt one; at the top right can be seen the beginnings of the lamented Bletchley Flyover, designed to speed transits from the north to the west, avoiding the nets and snares of London. It ran parallel to the main line for a while, past the station (the Bedford line joining it in the meantime) to cross the main line south of the station a few hundred yards behind where the photographer is standing for this view. It proved a white elephant and was abandoned after great cost but was still there at last look, quietly crumbling away.

Further north, Rugby was an altogether busier and more important operating centre and in the early 1960s was major industrial centre in its own right though September 1963 saw the last of the shed's Jubilees taken out of use and their work given over to Class 5s; one of them, 44833, leaves the station with a down class A train on 16 July 1963. An electric depot was established at Rugby in the middle of 1963, on the site of the old LNW Repair Shop.

Rugby was still busy with steam in the summer of 1963, though the EE Type 4s had the lion's share of the scheduled passenger trains. Pacifics and Scots and the rest were still plentiful, and there were still V2s to be seen rumbling over the viaduct at the south, or rather east of the station. The familiar backdrop is the old British Thomson Houston works, best known for its electrical systems and steam turbines. There had been a merger with Metropolitan-Vickers in the distant past but in 1960 they were merged by the holding company, Associated Electrical Industries (AEI). In this wonderful scene of 16 July 1963, two 8Fs, 48120 and 48361 amble along either off to shed or about to take up trains, with a third, 48345, behind.

Another 8F, 48020 with yet another freight north of the station, on 16 July 1963. The number of wagons illustrate the still relatively healthy level of traffic, though the sands were already shifting under BR's feet, as it were.

Stanier mogul 42958 (with that curious left-over lettering on the smokebox number plate – see *The Book of the Stanier 2-6-0s*, Irwell Press) leaves the station with a down freight on 6 July 1963; clear view of the magnificent No.5 signal box. The distant sidings were apparently called the 'exchange sidings'. The mogul has the rearranged lamp irons; to make work safer under the wires the top lamp was moved to the smokebox door and the middle buffer beam one shifted rightwards to match it.

Britannia 70001 LORD HURCOMB forges north (or rather west, the line lying on a largely east-west axis through the town) with a down class 4 freight at Rugby on 16 July 1963. With the wires creeping inexorably down from the north (they would reach Lichfield Trent Valley in a few weeks and electric working begin in October) Rugby, in the absence of any masts as yet, had a timeless steam age atmosphere; at least four other steam locos are at work in this picture.

Actually the masts were a lot closer than you'd think; *they're behind you...* as they say in panto. The photographer has simply turned left to photograph an incoming up train behind Class 5 44865; the masts, marching south, are not far behind...

One of Rugby's Jubilees, 45684 JUTLAND, put into store at the end of the summer season, at the station on 16 July 1963. Coaled up and in fair nick (for the time) it is serving as one of the station pilots; the other at this time, July-August, was 45723 FEARLESS. These were reported as the only *regular* duties for the local Jubilees; presumably as north and south pilot ready to cover failures and other emergencies. The shed yard is over there on the right.

8F 48646 comes in from the north with a coal train (you'd assume the wagons are loaded) in July 1963. A Royal Scot appears at the far left.

The same engine, 48646, around the same time. It hails from Bletchley and seems to be engaged in a spot of shunting on this occasion. With all this going on in time-honoured fashion there was a sense of life proceeding as it ever was; yet how quickly it would all disappear. The masts came, a veritable sea of them in fact, sidings went out of use, traffic disappeared and Rugby lost all its old junction quality. The grand station no longer matched the traffic and instead of signpost to the north the town is now part of the London commuter belt.

A brisk walk away from the rambling old LNW station was the altogether different ex-GC Rugby Central, more or less a country station and but a byway between Leicester and Marylebone. There was plenty going on too, on the GC; here on 16 July 1963 9F 92093 has a up train of what were 'Boplate' wagons which were intended for slab steel and suchlike, it would seem. The load certainly looks to be of that nature. The 9F has had it front lamp irons rearranged.

A Nottingham-Marylebone passenger train hurries by behind Annesley's 45334 near Rugby Central on 17 July 1963. There was a wide variety of motive power on the line at this time, though a lot of it wasn't in the best of health; these semi-fasts at the time could throw up Class 5s, B1s, Jubilees, V2s and Royal Scots while the same types would work the freights, along with 8Fs, WDs and 9Fs. A York B16 was by no means a rare sight.

The dying days of the 'windcutters' if you like; 92094 with down coal empties near Rugby Central in July 1963.

Back to the Midland station and an 8F in finest 'BR Grey' livery, a distinctive yet unpleasant 'default' look which took several months of dedicated neglect to perfect. It's 48656, just.

48221 clumps north with a freight in July 1963. This timeless scene was, as we know only too well, not long for this world. A few hundred yards away, back south at the side of the station, preparations were being made for the New Order. A new (it would be relatively short-lived, like much of the new operating infrastructure) Electric Depot was being fashioned from the old steam Repair Shops and an electric loco, E3054, was already in use for training, even though the OHL was still miles off, at Tamworth. Ingeniously, a length of siding had been equipped

with wires and energised and crews acquainted themselves with E3054 by, presumably, running it up and down the yard. How we overlooked all that wealth of wagon variety then, leading to an enjoyable mass of modelling detective work ever since. In fact modellers today probably very much underestimate the variety in regular use. Observe just the first four wagons of this train; a much-repaired old eight planker, a similarly patched-up steel open, an empty Conflat A and a low tarpaulined open. Marvellous.

This is Mirfield in Yorkshire, as the county was always called and should still be called. The walk along the Euston Road from Euston to St Pancras takes about five minutes and back in the 1960s, though Euston and the Arch were toppling into dust, the great blank walls of the doomed Somers Town goods depot were still there, pock-marked by shrapnel. It might have seemed impossibly remote but you'd have been confident of getting to Mirfield from Euston and go back on the Midland to St Pancras in one day. Opinions canvassed vary from 'easy' to 'bit of a marathon' to 'why, for just a load of old WDs?' It was another world back then, so much more so than today, when England is 'evened out' socially and culturally and the worse for it. We have uniform shops, banks, industrial units and anonymous homes so that apart from landscape it is often not immediately obvious where you are in the country. Once upon a time building styles and materials were distinctive even in different parts of the same county. No longer. Of moors, mines and mills, only the former is still there, eternal, in the towns and countryside once so associated with sheds like Mirfield. With the edge of town as backdrop, 4F 0-6-0s doze in the yard in July 1963. The main part of the roof used to be in the northlight pattern, like the portion over the offices and shops on the left, but was rebuilt by the LMS in this style in the 1930s

By the steaming sixties, the place had types that were rapidly becoming rare down south; 4Fs were disappearing, as were Crabs; 42733 stands in the shed yard on 25 July 1963.

A perfect place for spotting; a mass of fresh earthworks and assuredly mum(s) went bonkers that night. A WD 2-8-0, 90584, heads east past Mirfield shed with the usual deafening, clanging and banging, loose-coupled empty mineral wagons. The curious, incongruent, Victorian-Gothic pile on the left was the shed 'barracks' from the days of lodging turns. Observe the rake of coal wagons on the incline into the 'coal hole'; Mirfield shed retained this original Lancashire & Yorkshire feature to the end and was never provided with any mechanical coaling or ash disposal plant.

4F 0-6-0s (44422, nearest, was fresh off the Somerset & Dorset, from Templecombe) at Mirfield on 25 July 1963. The year had begun with Mirfield down to its last 4F so they were becoming ever more scarce in the district, giving way to hordes of WDs.

The view from the Woodend Road bridge, looking west towards Heaton Lodge Junction on 25 July 1963; coal empties hauled by Rose Grove's 90584. You can see some of the special 'speed' colour light signals originally introduced by the LMS in the 1930s, as well as more conventional signals at the junction in the distance. The girder bridge in the middle background carried the new line to Leeds over the River Calder and the canal, via Cleckheaton Spen, Gomersal and Gildersome to Farnley Junction. It closed to local passenger traffic in October 1953 but still served for main line trains until January 1966 – see also *In The Valley of the Calder, British Railways Illustrated*, Vol.17 No.5. The distinctive building on the skyline middle right is the 'Community of Resurrection', a famous training establishment for priests.

Double heading past the shed by York B1 61069 and Newton Heath Class 5 44696; the famous York-Manchester parcels on 25 July 1963. Though still very much 'LMS' in nature, this former L&Y territory had passed to the North Eastern Region in September 1956, with Mirfield recoded from 25D to 56D.

So it was that Mirfield would frequently play host to engines of LNER origin, and increasingly such types were actually allocated, though there was no rapid, wholesale replacement of the sort we saw when say, the LMR took over former WR sheds. It was thus no miracle to see B1s, K1s and even V2s on shed at Mirfield by this period but a remarkable circumstance was the allocation of six ex-NER B16 4-6-0s to the shed in November 1960. The B16s, traditionally, had been confined to two or three sheds, York for many years and then Neville Hill and Selby. This is 61461, stabled there on 25 July 1963 not long before its withdrawal.

Back to beefier London Midland roots and a Crab, Newton Heath's 42733 making its way west past the shed on 25 July 1963.

Yet another WD clumps east, past the shed at Mirfield on 8 June 1964, under Woodend Road which led from the shed entrance (note those steps down) to the town – the station was ten minutes walk away.

A splendid view east to the town, with a Jubilee, 45581 BIHAR AND ORISSA hauling a hotchpotch of vehicles, 8 June 1964. The Woodend Road bridge crosses the line and, just beyond, you can make out most of the eight roof pitches at the back of the shed. A better view, too, of some of the 'speed signalling'.

The shed yard and its 'coal hole' again, with this time what looks like a 9F inside being coaled. LM 2-6-4T 42149 rattles by with a westbound collection of vans.

We meet 42733 again, a year older and somewhat rustier, running east this time with coal empties, under the Woodend Road bridge on 8 June 1964. The portion of the shed at the right, as mentioned, are the original L&Y stores, offices and workshops, still in that company's distinctive northlight pattern style of roofing. The building and its yard had a colourful story after it was closed to steam in January 1967; first it served as a signing on/stabling point for diesels and after June 1967 the last rails were torn up and the place was used as a scrap yard. In the early 1970s part of the old yard was taken over for pig swill tankers, supplying an adjacent pig farm and with the prevailing easterlies, the good people of Mirfield were sorely tried. It closed in the early 1980s but the building was substantially intact until 2006, when the site was cleared for a housing development.

A diversion north – probably impossible in the real world of the 1960s – but impossible to resist, so charming is it. This the viaduct through Todmorden on 25 March 1966 (there is still snow on the 'tops') with a mineral train snaking its way across, northbound. The loco has just cleared the monumental, magnificent, castellated viaduct over the Rochdale Canal, part of which can be glimpsed to the right.

On the same day, there is time to hurry south to Sowerby Bridge, to find one of Mirfield's Black Fives, 45208 running light and in fair nick by the look of it.

An unusually bright 8F for the time, at Sowerby Bridge on 25 March 1966. 48062 has presumably been at Crewe of late; it is a Rose Grove engine and was still there during the 'last rites' months of 1968 though it was not preserved. See it at work for instance in *The Steaming Sixties No.3: The Shed and The Pit* by Paul Anderson.

Normanton now, on 20 March 1967. The last of the LM 2-6-4Ts were few and scattered, reduced to fifty or so engines scattered far and wide even by the beginning of the year and all were gone by the end of it. With a horrible daubed 55E (someone presumably had nicked the shed plate) 42083 represents the twilight of that noble institution, the steam station pilot.

The other half of Normanton's 2-6-4T stud, 42252, on 25 August 1967 and once again serving as Normanton station pilot. As such it must have been one of the last active members of the class; some months earlier it had been at Tebay, one of the banking engines, so life was a bit more leisurely for its last few months.

South to Leeds; we're pushing the possibilities of this itinerary – a lot – but a teatime/early evening departure from Leeds Central might get us home to St Pancras in time. This is the Holbeck triangle immediately north of Holbeck shed and just to the west of the City and Central stations; more specifically the north side in front of Monk Bridge Iron Works on 26 August 1967, with Holbeck's own 45428 running in with a train. The condition of the engine and the camera-wielding observers suggest a special; Holbeck would close to steam in a month or two.

On 31 August 1967 a Class 5 in more typical condition, 44896, comes round the north side of the triangle with an up parcels. The box is Whitehall Junction, a Midland structure built in 1908 to replace an earlier box of 1893. It seems in this view to have already been closed, with the inauguration of the recent Leeds power signalling in April 1967.

Light engine round the triangle: former Crosti 9F 92029, off Holbeck shed, on 31 August 1967.

And another; 45208 off the 'Devonian' on 31 August 1967. The photographer's notes record that the engine is retiring light to Low Moor shed, Bradford. This would make sense for it bears the short-lived final code for that shed, 55J. It had been 56F since the old LM Wakefield District had been absorbed into the NER in 1956 and, rather pointlessly (for it closed in September 1967) was reassigned to the Leeds District as 55J in June that year. There would not have been any shed plates cast for this, hence the daubing of the new code, on black square background – possibly uniquely, modellers note!

A splendidly filthy 44826 comes round with empty stock on 31 August 1967.

Mineral wagons trundling round the Holbeck triangle on the same day, 31 August 1967, behind 8F 48158, approaching oh so slowly then disappearing into the distance. And with that we must head south. Holbeck shed lay only a couple of hundred yards behind the photographer; it was a curious place by now, in its last year as a steam shed but where Jubilees and Britannias were still being repaired alongside Deltics.

On the way south, as a sample of life on the Midland, we pause at Derby to note Saltley's 44841 at the Midland station there, on 25 August 1961. It would certainly have been a straightforward affair to have got to Mirfield for the day from Euston around 1963-64, returning to St Pancras. A train off Euston about 8.30pm would have seen us in Manchester in time for a connection at 12.55pm (or thereabouts) to Leeds which arrived at Mirfield at 2.20pm. The spotter would have had just under two hours to do the shed and get back to the station for a 4.15pm stopper to Leeds (New) arriving at 4.55pm which gave a 25 minute connection from Leeds Wellington to St Pancras where the last train of the day arrived at 9.11pm – though it must be stressed, this is not intended as any sort of historical record. I put it forward as something desirable; a daydream, no more! Saying that, I'd be pleased to hear from any reader who could construct a plausible/provable itinerary. At this period Leeds New and Wellington were two parts of one establishment, soon to be turned into the one present day station, following the closure of the former GN terminus, Leeds Central.

Up from its Bristol home the same day, 45660 ROOKE takes water at Derby Midland station.

On the last leg back to London, and St Pancras; on 25 May 1963 44814 heads an up class C freight on the goods lines (the up slow) at Elstree. It had been a terrible winter, with derailments, diesel failures, ice and snow and day upon day of thick fog, reducing the Midland to chaos at times. Boiler failures on new Peaks saw the new Type 4s on freight trains and Jubilees and Class 5s turned out for the fast passenger trains. At one point towards the end of January trains had to be diverted to the slow lines at Ampthill while giant icicles were removed from the air shafts!

Up Cup Final special from Hinckley (the game was Leicester City versus Manchester United) behind 45617 MAURITIUS at Elstree on 25 May 1963. By this time the near monopoly of diesels, especially Peaks, had been restored, except for specials and reliefs along with some mineral trains. The Rugby League Cup Final (Wakefield Trinity versus Wigan – we started off at Euston with the 1964 game with the picture on page 2) had brought a gaggle of well turned out Jubilees but the FA Cup was disappointing in comparison, bringing out mainly Peaks and even a Wath Brush Type 2 D5808 on a special from Cudworth. Apart from 45617 there were apparently only two or three other steam hauled specials, behind a Jubilee (45611) a Black Five (see over) and a BR Class 5.

That same FA Cup Final, 25 May 1963, and Class 5 44981 comes south at Elstree, this time on the up fast. This special originated from Mansfield.

A Crab at Cricklewood shed; Burton's 42769 on 13 May 1961.

On 7 May 1960 the first of two unexpected circumstances saw DM 198717, the shed breakdown van of all things, derailed in the yard at Cricklewood Motive Power Depot. The second unexpected turn of events is that the locomotive to hand which is saving the day (it could have been anything) turns out to be a Shoeburyness three cylinder 2-6-4T off the LTS, 42500. From its fine condition it would surely be on its way back from Derby after overhaul.

Kentish Town shed on 14 June 1962 with 45611 HONG KONG parked outside; by now Jubilees were mainly a weekend sight. The previous winter had been a hard one though the disruptive diesel failures were just a curtain raiser on what was to come during the Arctic conditions of 1962-63. In a mirror image of events over on the LNW, at Willesden/Camden, Kentish Town, the Midland London passenger shed, was run down and closed while diesels were concentrated out at Cricklewood. The great roundhouses are still there however, preserved as the premises of a large building firm.

Back home; St Pancras on 19 September 1959 and Cricklewood's filthy black 2P 4-4-0 40580. It was an interesting period on the Midland, with Manchester expresses diverted from Euston, the new DMU local service (launched from January 1960) and the last gasp of 4-4-0s on piloting work. It is of some interest to note that the official announcement of the closure of poor St Pancras, long despised and neglected, came in the autumn of 1967, with services to be diverted to Euston via Nuneaton. The rest, as they say, is history...